AFRICA FOCUS

MODERN AFRICA

Rob Bowden and Rosie Wilson

Heinemann Library
Chicago, Illinois

www.heinemannraintree.com
Visit our website to find out
more information about
Heinemann-Raintree books.

To order:
☎ Phone 888-454-2279
💻 Visit www.heinemannraintree.com
to browse our catalog and order online.

Edited by Louise Galpine and Rachel Howells
Designed by Richard Parker and Manhattan Design
Original illustrations © Capstone Global Library Ltd
Illustrated by Oxford Designers and Illustrators
Picture research by Mica Brancic
Originated by Heinemann Library
Printed in the United States of America in Eau Claire, WI.
122214   008694RP

14 13 12
10 9 8 7 6 5 4 3

Library of Congress Cataloging-in-Publication Data
Wilson, Rosie.
  Modern Africa / Rosie Wilson and Rob Bowden.
    p. cm. -- (Africa focus)
  Includes bibliographical references and index.
  ISBN 978-1-4329-2438-6 (hc) -- ISBN 978-1-4329-2443-0
(pb)
  1. Africa--History. I. Bowden, Rob, 1973- II. Title.
  DT20.W55 2008
  960--dc22
                    2008048304

Acknowledgments
We would like to thank the following for permission to
reproduce photographs: Corbis pp. **19** (Gideon Mendel), **22**
(Bettmann), **29** (Ed Kashi), **30** (Patrick Durand/ Sygma),
31 (William Campbell/ Sygma), **32** (© Jeremy Hartley),
33 (Rob Taggart/ Reuters), **35** (Micheline Pelletier); Getty
Images pp. **7 & 15** (Paul Thompson/ FPG/ Stringer/Hulton
Archive), **10** (The Gallery Collection), **11** (James P. Blair/
National Geographic), **13** (Bentley Archive/ Popperfoto), **17**
(Gregg Cobarr/ WireImage), **18** (Sahm Doherty/ Time & Life
Pictures), **21** (William F. Campbell/ Time & Life Pictures),
23 (Keystone/ Stringer/ Hulton Archive), **24** (Christopher
Pillitz), **36** (AFP/ Timothy A Clark), **39** (Johnny Eggit/
AFP), **40** (Stephen Chernin/ Stringer); istockphoto.com p. **5**
(© Bruce Block); Lonely Planet Images p. **37** (Ariadne Van
Zandbergen); Mary Evans Picture Library p. **6**; Panos p. **32**
(© Jeremy Hartley); Photolibrary pp. **9, 26** (Caroline Penn);
The Bridgeman Art Library p. **12** (National Army Museum,
London).

Cover photograph of former political prisoner Nelson Mandela
campaigning for the presidency of South Africa, reproduced
with permission of Corbis (Peter Turnley).

We would like to thank Danny Block for his invaluable help in
the preparation of this book.

Every effort has been made to contact copyright holders of
material reproduced in this book. Any omissions will be
rectified in subsequent printings if notice is given to the
publishers.

All the Internet addresses (URLs) given in this book were valid
at the time of going to press. However, due to the dynamic
nature of the Internet, some addresses may have changed, or
sites may have changed or ceased to exist since publication.
While the author and Publishers regret any inconvenience this
may cause readers, no responsibility for any such changes can
be accepted by either the author or the Publishers.

Contents

Some words are printed in bold, **like this**. You can find out what they mean by looking in the glossary on page 44.

Africa Today

Modern Africa is a diverse **continent** made up of 53 countries. From the deserts in the north to the lush tropical forests of central Africa and the rich, high grasslands of eastern and southern Africa, each region has its own environment and characteristics. Its people are equally varied, with hundreds of languages and thousands of **ethnic groups**. Patterns of wealth, education, and health are just as wide-ranging, and make it difficult to talk about Africa as a single place. Nevertheless, nearly all countries in Africa have one thing in common—a history of control and domination from outside.

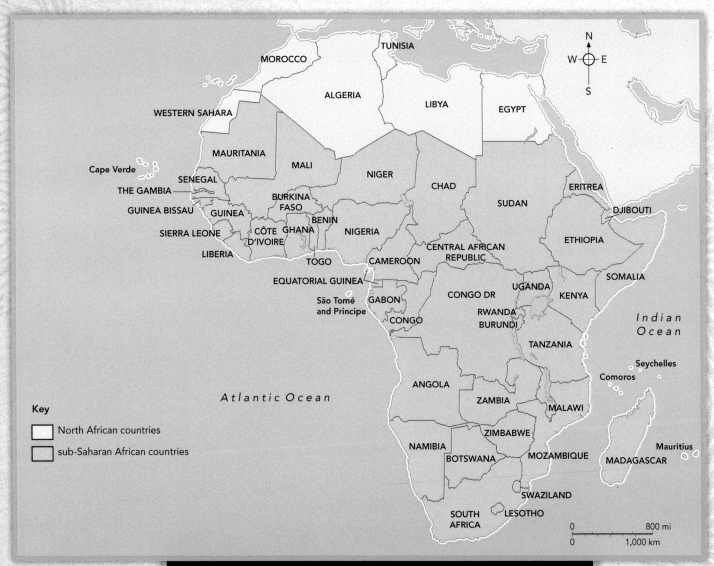

This map shows the continent of Africa as it is today. North Africa is separated from sub-Saharan Africa by the Sahara Desert. There are also differences in politics, culture, and language between the two regions.

A mysterious continent

Africa has a long and rich history. It is where humankind began, and it was home to some of the earliest human societies, such as the ancient Egyptians. For thousands of years, however, Africa remained a mystery to much of the rest of the world. Over time, parts of Africa's history and culture were revealed through **trade** links with the outside world, but these only told part of the story.

Colonial Africa

From the mid-1400s, when European explorers first arrived in Africa, **slavery** greatly weakened African societies and left them vulnerable to outsiders. European nations took advantage of this weakness and began to take direct control of Africa's **resources**. By the mid-1800s, European nations were in a rush to seize as much of Africa's minerals, wealth, and land as they could. This became known as the Scramble for Africa, and it continued until a conference in 1884–1885 in Berlin. At this meeting the European powers of the time divided Africa up among themselves. They gave no thought to existing African societies and created a map of Africa that has changed little since. Decisions made in Berlin triggered a century of rapid change in which Europeans and Africans struggled for control.

Africa is home to beautiful landscapes and many different types of animals. These elephants are walking toward a watering hole in Tanzania, East Africa.

Colonial Africa

By the 1500s stories of Africa's riches had attracted the interest of several European countries. Portugal, Great Britain, Spain, and France had become powerful oceangoing nations. They had already conquered lands in Asia, the Americas, and the Caribbean, and by the 1500s they had trading posts around Africa. Africa's riches began to flow across the oceans to Europe, but it was not only riches that the Europeans wanted—they also wanted Africa's people. By the end of the 1700s, an estimated 12 million Africans had been taken as slaves. Most of these people ended up in the Americas, where they were sold to work on European **plantations** growing cotton, sugar, tobacco, and coffee.

Europe takes control

By 1900 almost all of Africa was under European control, but different nations ruled their **colonies** in very different ways. France considered their colonies to be part of France and were quick to introduce the French language and **culture**. They also tried to learn about the cultures of the people they now controlled. Great Britain introduced English as a language and set up education, health, transport, and political systems based on its own. Great Britain never saw its colonies as part of Britain, so it appointed companies or governors to manage its colonies. In some colonies, such as Uganda, the British used local rulers to help them keep control.

Officials of the British East Africa Company make a treaty with the Kikuyu people of modern Kenya in 1897. The treaty allowed them to rule the region and make it a colony of Britain.

Railways

Many European nations built railways in their new colonies to help them **export** African goods to Europe. One of the most successful was the Uganda railway in East Africa. This was built by the British to transport cotton from Uganda to the port town of Mombasa, Kenya. The British brought in workers from India to help them build the railway between 1895 and 1903. When it was completed many of the workers stayed. Their **descendants** live in Kenya and Uganda today.

The Uganda–Mombasa railway was completed around 1915. It was built by the British to connect Uganda to the port in Mombasa, Kenya.

Changing lives

Life for many Africans changed dramatically as a result of European **colonization**. Some lost their lands, while others found their way of life under threat because Europeans believed it was **primitive** or backward. Europeans tried to make Africans live more like them by introducing European ways of dressing, living, and learning. Many Europeans believed they were helping to "civilize" Africans. They did not understand that many African ways of life were ideally suited to the local environment, and they did not respect African customs and traditions.

Making people work

Many Africans did not want to work for the Europeans. They had their own **economies** based on farming, **livestock**, and skills such as carpentry. But the Europeans needed workers for their farms, to build roads and railways, and to manage their colonies. By the time of **colonial** Africa, **slavery** had been banned. The Europeans, however, forced Africans to work for them in a different way. They introduced a "head **tax**." This meant that many Africans had little choice but to work for Europeans in order to earn money to pay the tax.

Before the introduction of head taxes, many Africans lived without the need for money. They exchanged goods or services with one another. Land, too, was often not owned by individuals, but belonged to entire communities or tribes. This was known as common land. The introduction of taxes created a need for money. This forced people to take jobs on European-owned farms or to sell land to Europeans for little cost. Others found work in European homes and factories. The arrival of money in the African economy was to change the way things worked forever.

Africa Fact

Money has been used in parts of Africa for more than 1,000 years, but instead of coins, shells and beads were once used as a currency (money) to buy things.

Many Africans were forced to work for European colonists as servants or gardeners or in similar types of jobs. This photograph shows two African servants posing with their European master.

Colonial curiosity

Europe's colonization of Africa created a lot of curiosity among ordinary Europeans. Exhibitions of African art and wildlife brought back from the **continent** would attract large crowds. To many Europeans, Africa seemed strange and fascinating. It was certainly very different from Europe. European artists, writers, and musicians were inspired by Africa, but relatively few had the chance to visit the continent or talk to Africans. As a result, the ideas represented in their works were often not very accurate and led to many **stereotypes** about Africa and its people.

A hungry lion attacks an antelope in a 1905 painting by Henri Rousseau. Rousseau was interested in jungle animals and plants from Africa, but he had never left France.

The safari

For those who could afford it, Africa became a thrilling tourist destination. The main attraction was its wildlife and the opportunity to hunt wild and dangerous beasts. Wealthy Europeans and Americans traveled to eastern and southern Africa for organized hunting trips. A hunting trip became known as a *safari*, which means "journey" in the Swahili language of East Africa. Safaris are popular in parts of Africa today, but people do not hunt the animals. They take photographs of them instead.

Independent Africa

Ethiopia is an unusual African country. It was one of only two countries (the other was Liberia) that was not colonized by Europeans. Italy occupied Ethiopia for a short period between 1936 and 1941 and forced its leader, the Emperor Haile Selassie, to flee to England. During World War II, however, Britain helped Haile Selassie to recover control of Ethiopia, and the Italians quickly surrendered. Selassie's strength against European colonizers made him a hero in other parts of Africa that wanted to be independent from Europe.

Haile Selassie was popular with his people. He ensured that ordinary Ethiopians benefited from foreigners growing coffee on Ethiopian land by making all foreigners work with a local partner.

AFRICA FACT

People who follow the Rastafari religious movement believe that Haile Selassie was the second coming of Christ. They believe that he is still alive and will one day lead all African people to a promised land.

Struggle for Freedom

At the time of **colonization**, Africa was not a strong **continent**. Almost four centuries of **slavery** had destroyed many communities and led others into **civil war**. These communities presented little opposition to the more powerful and well-equipped European forces. Any opposition was in most cases easily defeated by European armies.

In this 1825 painting, British forces attack the Asante people of West Africa. Although the painting shows the Asante as weak, they continued to fight the British throughout the 1800s.

Resisting colonization

Despite their weakened state, very few Africans welcomed European control of their lands. This opposition was sometimes shown through direct force, such as the Zulu resistance against British control of South Africa in 1879. The Zulu were at first successful, but were eventually defeated by Britain's greater military strength. France faced similar opposition movements in West Africa, as did Germany in Tanzania.

Resistance to **colonial** rule did not always take place through fighting, however. Tricks such as cutting telegraph wires were used to disrupt communications between the African **colonies** and Europe. Food, water, and other supplies were also disrupted to make life difficult for colonial leaders.

The Mau Mau

The Kikuyu people of Kenya were one of many **ethnic groups** whose land was taken by Europeans during the colonial period. In the 1940s a group of Kikuyu formed a movement that became known as the Mau Mau. The Mau Mau wanted to win back their lands. Beginning in 1952, they launched violent attacks against British settlers and Kikuyu who were loyal to the British. As the attacks became worse, the British announced a **state of emergency** and fought back.

This photograph of Jomo Kenyatta was taken in 1952, around the time when the Mau Mau began its actions against European settlers. Kenyatta was arrested because the British said he was a Mau Mau leader. He later became the first president of Kenya.

Between 1952 and 1956, at least 11,500 Kikuyu and Mau Mau fighters were killed in the fighting. A further 20,000 Kikuyu were arrested by the British and placed in **detention camps**. Only 32 British settlers were killed by the Mau Mau, but the violence shocked Britain and eventually led to Kenya's **independence** in 1963.

13

Africa and the World Wars

World War I (1914–1918) and World War II (1939–1945) both had major effects on Africa. They turned colonial powers against one another and led to direct fighting on the African continent. When Germany lost World War I, its African colonies (modern-day Tanzania, Togo, and Cameroon) were surrendered to France and Britain. In World War II, Egypt, Tunisia, and Somalia became major battlegrounds between Britain and its **allies** on one side and Germany, Italy, and its allies on the other.

More than two million Africans took part in World War I, and 500,000 fought in World War II. They fought mainly in Africa or worked as carriers for European forces, transporting supplies and taking away the injured. More than 170,000 Africans died fighting for their colonial masters. Those who survived to return home believed that European nations owed them for their **sacrifices**. Anger grew among many Africans, and more and more people began to call for independence from Europe.

African soldiers

"He told us we were going to the Great War [World War I] to help the king's soldiers who were preventing the Germans coming to our country and burning it. We left and marched far into the bush."

Recruit no.1,475, quoted from the BBC Story of Africa, 2001.

A weakened master

By the end of World War II, Europe had been greatly weakened. Many towns and cities were in ruins because of the fighting, and millions of people had been killed or injured. The cost of rebuilding their own countries made it hard for European nations to meet the cost of rebuilding their colonies, too. Africans who had fought with the Europeans realized that their colonial masters were now weak. They used their experience as soldiers to organize groups that could fight for independence from their weakened masters.

African soldiers were pictured recovering in a hospital in Dinan, France, during World War I.

The Suez Crisis

In 1956 President Nasser of Egypt took control of the Suez Canal, the main waterway between the Mediterranean Sea and the Red Sea. It provided a short cut to Asia for travelers from Europe and America, since they did not need to sail around Africa.

The canal was built between 1859 and 1869 by the Suez Canal Company. In 1956 the company was mainly owned by Britain. When Nasser took control of the canal, Britain, France, and Israel attacked Egypt and occupied the land around the canal. The **United Nations** stepped in to prevent the fighting. Britain, France, and Israel were forced to pull out, and the canal remained in Egyptian control, where it remains today. The defeat was embarrassing for Britain and France. It was seen as a sign of Europe's weakening control of its African colonies.

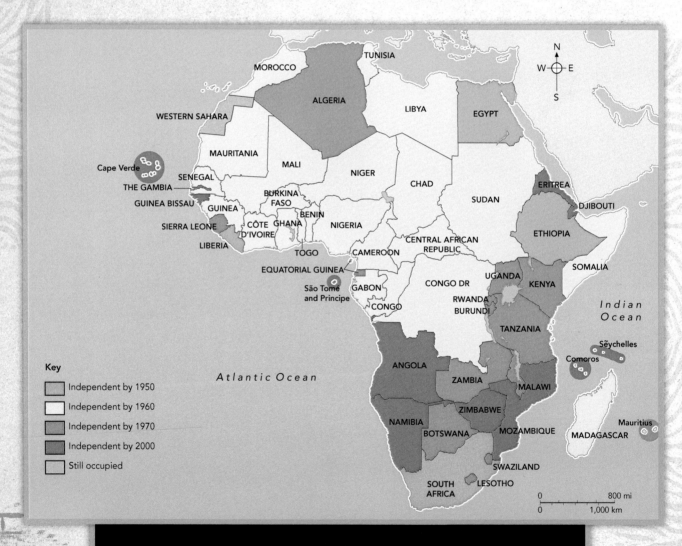

Key
- Independent by 1950
- Independent by 1960
- Independent by 1970
- Independent by 2000
- Still occupied

This map shows the different decades when African countries gained independence from their colonial rulers.

The beginning of the end

In 1957 Ghana became the first colony in sub-Saharan Africa to win its independence from Europe (in this case Britain). Ghana's first president, Kwame Nkrumah, said, "Africa must unite!" He believed that if Africans worked together then all of Africa could become independent from Europe. Other leaders, including Haile Selassie of Ethiopia, Jomo Kenyatta of Kenya, Gamal Abdel Nasser of Egypt, and Julius Nyerere of Tanzania, joined Kwame Nkrumah as powerful voices calling for an end to colonialism in Africa.

A wave of independence

In the 1960s a wave of independence swept quickly across Africa when European nations wanted to bring their control of African colonies to an end. Between 1960 and 1962, 23 African countries became independent of European countries. More followed, until by 1970 only a handful of countries were still colonized. These included Portugal's colonies of Angola, Mozambique, Guinea Bissau, Cape Verde, and São Tomé and Principe. These nations finally gained their independence between 1973 and 1975, after violent struggles with the Portuguese.

The Jamaican reggae singer Bob Marley used some of his songs to call for the independence of African nations. Shortly before he died in 1981, he was invited to sing at the Zimbabwean independence celebrations.

Apartheid in South Africa

Apartheid means "keep apart." It was the name given to laws introduced by the white South African government from 1948 to 1994. In South Africa, English and Dutch settlers had taken much of the best land for themselves. They introduced apartheid laws to prevent black South Africans from threatening their control. Nonwhites could only live in certain areas and could not get good jobs. Their movements were strictly controlled by identity documents, and they were not allowed to vote. Black South Africans were even forced to learn Afrikaans, the language of white South Africans.

Apartheid was criticized by people around the world. Two men who led these protests were Stephen Biko and Nelson Mandela.

Supporters of Stephen Biko hold up his picture outside the building where the enquiry into how he died was taking place.

Stephen Biko (1946—1977)

Stephen Biko was a **campaigner** for the rights of black South Africans during apartheid. The white government considered him to be a threat, and Biko was arrested on many occasions. Following one of these arrests in 1977, Stephen Biko died after spending 24 days in prison. Doctors who examined his body said he died of head injuries and had probably been beaten. At the time the police said nothing about this, but in 1997 five police officers admitted that they had beaten Biko to death.

NELSON MANDELA

Nelson Mandela was a key member of the African National Congress (ANC) who protested against apartheid. In 1960 the ANC was banned, but its members continued to protest and plan ways to **sabotage** the government. In 1962 Mandela was imprisoned, and in 1964 he was **sentenced** to life imprisonment for **treason** and sabotage. While in prison Mandela became a symbol for the international struggle to end apartheid, and there were even songs calling for his freedom. In 1990 he was freed by South African President F.W. de Klerk and worked with the president to bring an end to apartheid. In 1994 South Africa had its first-ever **free elections**, and Mandela became president.

Nelson Mandela stands next to the former president of South Africa in 1994. They received the Nobel Peace Prize for their work in ending apartheid and bringing peace to South Africa.

An Independent Africa

When African nations became **independent** from European nations, they had to decide on new names. The Kenya Protectorate became Kenya, for example, after Mount Kenya in the center of the country. The table below shows some of the other names that were chosen for newly independent African nations and what they mean.

Name of country	Where the name came from
Angola	Named after Ngola, the king of the people living in the region when the Portuguese arrived.
Ghana	Named after the ancient West African kingdom of the same name that traded in salt and gold.
Mali	Named after the Mali kingdom in West Africa—a great **civilization** many years before Europeans came.
Somalia	Named after the Somalis—the main ethnic group in Somalia.
Zambia	Named after the Zambezi River, which flows through the country.
Zimbabwe	Named after the ancient city of Great Zimbabwe, which **traded** as far away as China.

Beginning to lead

Independence gave Africans hope for the future. However, new political leaders had little experience in running a country, and there were arguments about who should control land and how to share wealth. In many new countries, the borders chosen by **colonial** powers divided **ethnic groups**, and in some cases forced enemy ethnic groups to live alongside one another. Border problems caused further tensions in many young African nations.

Many violent changes

The early years of Africa's independence were marked by violent clashes when different groups struggled for power. In the 1960s Africa had 21 **coups**, where the government of a country was suddenly overthrown. This was normally done by the army using force and imprisoning or killing leaders. At least another 40 coups took place in the 1970s and 1980s. Armies took control with the promise of improving things, but in many instances things became worse because the army would use force to control people. Sometimes soldiers and generals even stole money from people and threatened them.

Julius Nyerere was president of Tanzania between 1964 and 1985. He was respected as a leader and was a founder of the Organization of African Unity in 1963. His speeches and actions have inspired many other African leaders.

AFRICA FACT

Until the mid-1990s, 14 African leaders had been **assassinated**, with eight more murdered or **executed** after coups that forced them from power.

Nigerian-Biafran War

In several regions of Africa, groups of people have fought against unfair leaders and sometimes tried to break away to create countries of their own.

In Nigeria, many Igbo people were murdered as a result of violence within the country. In 1967 the Igbo people moved east and announced the new state of Biafra. The Nigerian government fought to regain control of Biafra in a war that lasted two-and-a-half years. Many Igbo people died during the fighting, but even more (at least half a million) died from starvation. This was because Nigeria blocked food supplies from reaching the people of Biafra and caused a **famine**.

A child suffers from severe malnutrition because of food shortages caused by the Nigerian–Biafra War.

AFRICA FACT

Twenty-three African countries have been run by an army. In 1975 a total of 14 African countries had military leaders.

Bloodshed

Most coups happened when leaders did not bring about the changes they had promised, or when the leadership of a country favored one ethnic group. Some handovers were peaceful and only affected the top leaders in government, but many were violent and affected ordinary people. Sierra Leone, Nigeria, Mozambique, and Uganda are all examples of this. In the Democratic Republic of the Congo and Sudan, political violence between different groups continues today. This is partly due to old rivalries, but is also about the control of **resources** such as oil and **minerals**.

IDI AMIN

Idi Amin commanded the Ugandan army, but in 1971 he led a coup and took control of the whole country. He was at first welcomed, but he began to use the force of the military to terrorize those who disagreed with his decisions. Thousands of people were arrested or killed. In 1978 Amin invaded neighboring Tanzania, but the Tanzanian army fought back. Amin fled to Libya and then to Saudi Arabia, where he died in 2003.

These Ugandan Asians are arriving at an airport in London. Idi Amin forced Asians who had settled in Uganda to leave the country, and he seized their homes, factories, and land.

The poverty trap

Following independence, many African governments struggled to meet the needs of their people. Their systems of trade, based on selling **raw materials** such as minerals and **crops**, had been set up during the colonial period to benefit European countries. Many African nations had no other way to make money and therefore continued with these systems. They thought they could become richer by growing more crops, so land was used to grow crops for **export** (known as cash crops) instead of local use. Unfortunately, the increased crop production led to lower prices, and African nations became poorer and poorer. They did not have enough money to build factories of their own and sell higher-priced goods. By 1990 many African nations were trapped in poverty and had less food available per person than they had when they became independent.

A Kenyan coffee picker sorts through beans while other women wait with their loads. Coffee is a major cash crop in East Africa, but low global prices keep many workers poor.

This graph shows how Africa's population has almost quadrupled (become four times bigger) between 1950 and 2000.

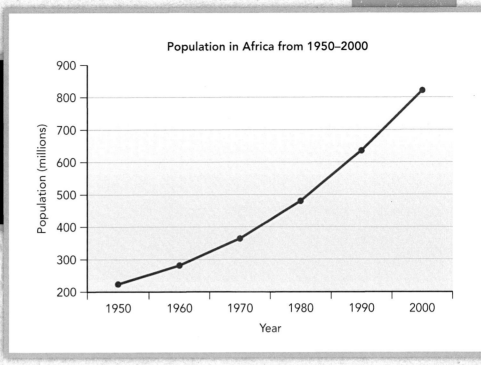

Population in Africa from 1950–2000

Too many people?

Africa's population was the fastest-growing in the world in the late-1900s. The poverty of governments meant that there were shortages of food, housing, education, and health care. People began to talk about "Africa in crisis," because things were getting worse and worse for the **continent**. Africa's population growth was often blamed, but others blamed unfair systems of trade that benefited wealthier nations and kept Africans in poverty.

Famine and aid

The problems in Africa became the focus of the world in the 1980s, when a series of famines caused hundreds of thousands of people to die. These were caused by a mixture of bad government, conflict, growing populations, and failed rains. An international campaign raised millions of dollars to provide food **aid** in countries such as Ethiopia and Sudan. People around the world began to ask questions about how this had happened.

AFRICA FACT

Despite population problems, many Africans believe that large families are a blessing and a sign of power and wealth.

Changing Life

Despite the troubles Africa has experienced since **independence**, there have been positive changes, too. Improvements in health care have reduced the number of children dying from diseases, for example, and more African children are educated now than ever before. North African countries such as Libya, Tunisia, Morocco, and Egypt now have standards of health and education similar to those of southern Europe.

This nurse is giving out medicine in a child welfare clinic in Ghana. Health facilities have greatly improved in some parts of Africa.

Moving to the cities

One of the biggest changes in Africa since the 1950s has been the rapid growth of its cities. Millions of people have left **rural** areas and abandoned farming in the hope of finding better jobs in Africa's cities. Between 1950 and 1985, the population of Africa's towns and cities doubled, and many are growing even faster today. Cities such as Cairo, Egypt, and Nairobi, Kenya, have grown so fast that there is a shortage of housing for everyone. Millions of Africans live in poor-quality areas known as **slums**. These are overcrowded and lack facilities such as toilets and schools.

Africa Fact

Cairo was the largest city in Africa in 2005, with more than 11 million people living there. It was larger than London, Chicago, or Beijing.

The newest killer

By the end of the 1900s, Africa was facing a major new challenge. A killer disease called **HIV/AIDS** was spreading quickly in **sub-Saharan Africa**. The populations of South Africa, Botswana, and Swaziland were most affected. There is no cure for the disease, and for many years people did not know what to do about it or even how it was spread. It is now known that it is spread by unsafe sex or **infected** blood, but there is still no cure.

The **United Nations** and other organizations have begun education programs to prevent people from becoming infected. A successful education plan in Uganda has helped to reduce the number of people catching the disease.

Africa's economy

Most people in Africa still work in farming of some sort, but farming has become less important as a source of **income**. As cities grew, factories opened and produced goods for local use and **export**. Tunisia, for example, has become an important clothes producer, and South Africa produces a wide range of **manufactured** goods. Many other jobs are in services such as teaching, banking, and tourism.

Black gold

Some of Africa's strongest **economies** are built on oil, which is sometimes called "black gold" because it is so valuable. Libya, Nigeria, Algeria, and Egypt all have large oil **resources** and made lots of money from selling oil to **Western** countries in the 1980s. But when oil prices went down, Nigeria's economy was in trouble. Global prices are not controlled by Africa, which makes oil production risky, just like farming. Another problem with oil production is that it is controlled by a small group of wealthy people, often with close links to the government and international oil companies. This means that local people do not benefit from the oil wealth. Some local people have even lost their land because oil companies want to reach the oil beneath it.

New opportunities

As the economy of Africa grows stronger, new opportunities for trade have appeared. Some of the richer countries, including South Africa, Nigeria, and Egypt, have a longer history of business, but during the 1990s other countries began to catch up.

AFRICA FACT

Eskom is an electricity company that was started by the South African government in 1923. It is now one of South Africa's most successful companies and has grown rapidly since the end of **apartheid**. During apartheid the company was not allowed to provide electricity to black South Africans, but it now has a policy to deliver "electricity for all." Eskom has used its expertise in electricity to work in other parts of Africa, too.

These workers are drilling for gas in the Niger Delta region of Nigeria. This region is rich in oil and gas, and has brought great wealth to Nigeria.

Dishonest leaders

Some African leaders have used their power to make themselves (and often their friends and family) very rich. This is called **corruption**. In the worst cases it has involved directly stealing the country's money.

Mobutu Sese Soko, the President of Zaire (now the Democratic Republic of the Congo), stole billions of dollars of the country's money. The money came from selling minerals such as copper. If people argued with him about what he was doing, he would simply **bribe** them with money to keep quiet. Mobutu was eventually forced from power in 1997, but by then corruption had become an everyday way of life. It remains a major problem in the Democratic Republic of the Congo today.

Mobutu Sese Soko is pictured sitting in his palace, wearing a leopard-skin hat. He became known as one of Africa's richest and most corrupt leaders.

Success stories: music and fashion

The movement of large numbers of people to African cities has led to exciting new **urban cultures**. These grew as different groups mixed and shared their traditions and ideas for the future. In the urban communities of South Africa, Kenya, Nigeria, and Congo, new music trends developed. An example of this is *Kwaito* music from South Africa, which mixes African drumming rhythms with heavy bass lines (low, rhythmic notes), and rapping. New fashions also developed when young people in cities started mixing Western-style clothing with bright African fabrics and designs.

Still struggling

The **famines** in Africa in the mid-1980s and again in the 1990s were a reminder that, for millions of Africans, life did not improve much in the 20th century. Hunger and poverty were still a major problem in many countries and had become worse in some. The population was still growing fast, too, with countries such as Uganda and Rwanda expected to double their populations in less than 25 years. This would place more pressure on Africa and bring about even more changes.

These refugees are fleeing the effects of famine in Ethiopia.

Developing Africa

African societies had survived for thousands of years without the help of outsiders, but when Europeans arrived they began to make it their business to help Africa. Some of the very first Europeans to settle in Africa were **missionaries**. They believed it was their duty to teach Africans how to live like Christians back in Europe. Throughout the 1900s, **Western** nations followed similar beliefs and felt that Africa needed to develop—to catch up with the West. This led to what is known as **aid**. This could be in the form of direct help, such as sending doctors or teachers to work in Africa, but was normally about giving or lending money.

These farmworkers are planting trees along a stone line, which is used to capture rainfall and prevent soil erosion.

Success stories: stone lines

In Burkina Faso in West Africa, local people worked with Oxfam, an international aid organization, to create a successful aid project. The soil in Burkina Faso was often baked hard by the hot sun there, which caused rainwater to flow across the soil instead of sinking into it. This meant that the soil was too hard for people to grow food. In 1974 local farmers started piling up stones to block the water and stop it running away, so that it would sink into the ground. Oxfam worked with the farmers to improve this method and train others how to do it. Soon, farmers across Burkina Faso were using stone lines to capture rainfall and allow crops to grow.

Some of the world's most famous music performers gathered onstage in London in 1985 to perform for Live Aid and raise money for victims of famine in Africa.

AFRICA FACT

In 1985 a musician named Bob Geldof organized rock music concerts in London and Philadelphia to raise money for Ethiopian **famine** victims. One hundred and eighty thousand people went to the concerts, and 1.5 billion people watched on television all over the world. The total amount of money raised by both concerts was around $280 million.

Turkwell Dam

Some aid projects have failed because of a lack of understanding about the problems they aim to solve, or because aid workers have not talked to local people enough. Other projects have experienced problems because of **corrupt** leaders.

The Turkwell Gorge Dam in Kenya is an example of this. The dam was planned to provide electricity, but was built in an area with low rainfall and a high risk of earthquakes. Studies said it was a bad idea, but the Kenyan government went ahead with the plans anyway. Many believe they were given money by the building company to make sure the dam continued. The dam was finished, but has never worked as it should. It only produces around half the planned amount of electricity.

Aid dependency

The belief that Africans need help from outside has led to what is known as aid dependency, in some parts of the **continent**. This is when governments or people rely too heavily on aid from outside and do little about problems themselves. Communities that become used to food handouts, for example, have been known to stop growing their own food and rely on the food aid instead. Food given as aid can even be taken to be sold in local markets to earn money. Some African governments have also become dependent on aid and borrowed large amounts that they are now struggling to pay back. Some people believe that Africa would be better off by trying to help itself.

SUCCESS STORIES: GREEN BELT KENYA

In 1977 members of the National Council for Women of Kenya were becoming concerned about the damage to the Kenyan environment and especially the loss of forests. They began an organization called the Green Belt Movement to organize tree-planting and educate people to protect the environment. They have also campaigned to protect forests and other environments from being further damaged. Between them, the women of the Green Belt Movement have planted more than 20 million trees!

Wangari Maathai founded the Green Belt Movement to work with Kenyan women, protect forests, and promote conservation.

Skills for Africa

The president of Uganda, Yoweri Museveni, thinks Africa is weak because it needs more skills. He has said that with better science, technology, and management skills, the continent would be able to "walk" by itself. Industries and businesses would develop and Africa would not need to depend on the rest of the world for help. Africa has made progress in building its skills, but many of the continent's most skilled workers leave Africa. Many African countries were poorer in 2000 than they were in 1990.

AFRICA'S AID DEPENDENCY

"Africa is like a man who falls and cannot get up on his own but has, instead, to wait for someone to help him get up and walk him."

(Yoweri Museveni, president of Uganda, speaking in 1986)

Yoweri Museveni, the president of Uganda, addresses the United Nations General Assembly in 2008.

This village of the Dogon people is in Mali, West Africa. African skills and knowledge about working with the environment have existed for centuries.

Learning from Africa

Many of the skills that Africa has always had are now becoming valued outside Africa. Because of a lack of money to buy chemicals, for example, African farmers have become expert **organic** farmers. Organic farming is becoming more popular in other parts of the world, and many lessons are being learned from African methods and ideas.

Barriers to progress

Even when local skills and local ideas are used to help improve life for Africans, there are many barriers to progress. These are some of the main ones:

Global **trade** rules allow countries in the **European Union (EU)** and countries such as the United States and Japan to pay farmers to grow **crops**. This allows farmers to sell crops for less than African farmers, even though they cost more to produce.

Africa's climate and environment means it has a naturally high risk of disasters such as flooding, **drought**, and disease.

HIV/AIDS is causing millions of deaths every year. Many of those dying are workers and parents. This is damaging many African **economies**. In addition, changes to the world's climate have already affected regions of Africa more than other places, causing greater risk of crop failures and famine.

Africa in the World

A look back at Africa's recent history shows that the world has benefited more from Africa than Africa has from the world. Great wealth has been created in nations outside Africa because they used African **resources** for their own benefit. African **independence** did not really change these patterns. Many would say that Africa is still not benefiting as much as it should from its relationship with the rest of the world.

Global **trade** and political systems were set up to benefit **Western** nations and help them rebuild their **economies** after World War II (1939–1945). Although these countries are now strong again, the systems that helped them have changed very little. When African countries won their independence, they felt free, but did not realize that they were still trapped by global systems.

Result of African freedom in the 1900s	Hidden trap
Independent nations with their own government.	African nations do not have money, so must borrow from wealthier nations who tell them what to do with the money.
Joined global organizations such as the **United Nations (UN)**.	African nations have no real power to make changes because wealthier nations have more control.
Traded with rest of world.	Caught in a "poverty trap," African nations had to buy costly imports and sell their own goods for low prices.
Had the opportunity to live and work abroad.	Africans were paid less than other workers abroad, and there was a loss of skilled workers in Africa.

Africa's debt

When they became independent, many African nations were offered **loans** by Western nations and international organizations such as the World Bank. These loans were supposed to be used to help Africa develop, but many African countries could not develop fast enough to pay back the loans. By the late 1990s, Africa was in massive **debt** and was paying more back in loan payments than it was receiving in new **aid**.

In 1985 the then-president of Tanzania, Julius Nyerere, said: "We cannot pay. You know it … should we really let our people starve so that we can pay our debts?"

Campaigners gather outside the G8 summit of world leaders in England in 1998. They were campaigning for Africa's debts to be reduced or dropped.

AFRICA FACT

In 1980 Africa owed $60 billion in loan repayments, but by 2000 this had grown to $212 billion.

Peace gone wrong

In 1992 the United Nations sent an American-led peacekeeping force into Somalia, in eastern Africa. Their aim was to stop the fighting between rival **ethnic groups** in the country, but the mission went badly wrong. Many peacekeepers were killed, and the UN began withdrawing its troops in March 1994.

Violence in Rwanda

Just one month later, violence erupted between the Hutu and Tutsi people in Rwanda. The United Nations seemed unsure of what to do after the experience of Somalia, and the United States and Europe refused to send any troops to Rwanda. More than a million people were killed during the violence, which lasted for almost five months. These events shocked people around the world.

A turning point

Also in 1994 Nelson Mandela became president of South Africa, and **apartheid** ended. This provided great hope, not just for South Africa but also for the whole African **continent**. Mandela spoke about Africans coming together and leaving the past behind.

A global presence

The 1990s did see an increased global presence for Africa. Two African leaders became Secretary-Generals for the United Nations—Boutros Boutros-Ghali from Egypt in 1992, and Kofi Annan from Ghana in 1997. They were able to use their position to remind world leaders of the need to help Africa solve its problems. Africa was also taking action and began to make plans for a new and stronger **African Union (AU)**. A global campaign to forgive Africa's debts was also started in the 1990s and had support from ordinary people across the world.

Kofi Annan was the Secretary-General of the United Nations between 1997 and 2007. Here he is talking at a UN meeting to raise money for Liberia after years of war.

Hope for the 21st century

As the 20th century came to a close, Africa still faced many challenges. These included **HIV/AIDS**, and the conflicts in Darfur (Sudan) and the Democratic Republic of the Congo. But there was also reason for hope. African **economies** had begun to show signs of growth for the first time in almost 30 years. In some countries, poverty had started to fall, too. Most importantly, Africa was now a continent of independent and mainly peaceful nations. It was able to put a century of turmoil and change behind it and plan for a brighter future.

Timeline

1807–1860 The transatlantic slave **trade** ends after 400 years and around 12 million people being shipped from Africa to the Americas.

1865 **Slavery** ends in the United States.

1879 The British-Zulu War is fought between the British Empire and the Zulu Empire.

1884–1885 European nations meet at the Berlin Conference to divide Africa into **colonies** and agree **trade** rules concerning the **continent**.

1896–1901 The Uganda railway is built, mostly by Indian workers.

1914–1918 More than two million Africans take part in World War I.

1939–1945 500,000 African men fight in World War II.

1952–1956 The Mau Mau conflict in Kenya takes place.

1956 The Suez Crisis occurs, and President Nasser of Egypt takes control of the Suez Canal. Britain, France, and Israel attack Egypt, and leave when the **United Nations (UN)** intervenes.

1957 Kwame Nkrumah becomes Ghana's first president when it achieves **independence**.

1963 Kenya becomes independent.

1960–1975 A wave of independence takes place in many African countries—see map on page 16.

1967–1970 Nigerian-Biafran War is fought when the Igbo people of Nigeria declared an independent state of Biafra.

1977 Stephen Biko, an activist against **apartheid**, dies in police custody in South Africa.

1979 Idi Amin, then president of Uganda, invades Tanzania. Defeated, he flees to Libya.

1980 Africa's population reaches 480 million.

1984 **HIV/AIDS** is found to be widespread in Africa.

1984–1986 Widespread famine in the African continent is caused by climate and lack of food because fertile land is used to grow cash crops instead of food crops.

1992 Boutros Boutros-Ghali becomes Secretary-General of the UN.

1992–1994 UN force led by the United States attempts to bring peace to warring ethnic groups in Somalia, but many are killed.

1994 South Africa ends the apartheid era, and Nelson Mandela is elected as the country's first black leader.

1994 Fighting between the Hutu and Tutsi **ethnic groups** in Rwanda leads to more than one million deaths.

1995 South Africa's Truth and Reconciliation Commission begins to repair the damage done by apartheid. It is chaired by Bishop Desmond Tutu and continues working until 1998.

1996 Uganda announces the introduction of its Universal Primary Education (UPE) program. It will pay for up to four children in every family to have free elementary education.

1997 Kofi Annan becomes Secretary-General of the UN.

1998 One in six of the world's children lives in Africa.

Glossary

African Union (AU) organization of 53 African countries that was launched in 2002 to promote development in the continent

aid support given to another country in the form of food, supplies, or money

ally nation that is united with another by political beliefs or that fights with another country on the same side during war

apartheid system of separation introduced by the white South African government in 1948. Nonwhite people were sent to separate schools and had separate transport. The system ended in 1994.

assassinate to kill a political or public figure with a surprise attack

bribe to offer a person money or other goods to persuade them to do what you want

campaigner person who attempts to achieve better conditions

civilization society with a high level of art, science, and government

civil war war fought within a country between different groups

colonial state of being a country that belongs to another country

colonization taking control of another country

colony land controlled by another country

continent one of the main areas of land on Earth. Many countries may be found on one continent.

corruption use of power to threaten or cheat on others who are less powerful

coup taking of power from a government or leader by swift and effective means

crop plant grown for use by people, such as cereals or vegetables

culture actions and beliefs of a society

debt money owed to an individual or organization

descendant relative of a particular person or group of people

detention camp place where prisoners are held temporarily

drought when there is little or no rainfall over a long time, causing water shortages

economy system under which a country creates, sells, and buys products

ethnic group people who share culture and language

European Union (EU) group of 27 countries in Europe with close political, economic, legal, and social ties

execute to put someone to death

export goods sold to another country; to sell to another country

famine severe food shortages causing starvation

free election election in which all citizens are able to vote

HIV/AIDS the disease AIDS is caused by the virus HIV. The virus attacks the body's ability to protect against infection. There is no cure for HIV or AIDS.

import goods bought by another country; to buy from another country

income money earned through work

independence freedom of a country to make its own laws and decisions

infected caught a disease

livestock animals kept for use or profit, such as farm animals

loan money lent to a person or country, to be returned by an agreed date and for a fee

manufactured made by humans

mineral nonorganic natural substance found in the earth

missionary person sent overseas to spread their religion

organic natural substance

plantation big farm where crops are grown by people who live and work there

primitive basic

raw material natural resource before it is processed by machines

resource mineral or raw material used by industry or government for goods or services

rural relating to life in the country

sabotage destroy, damage, or disrupt

sacrifice give something up in order to achieve a goal of greater importance

sentenced charged for a crime in a court of law and given an appropriate punishment

slavery practice of owning a slave

slum city area characterized by overcrowding and poor living conditions

state of emergency time of crisis declared by a government, during which normal laws can be stopped

stereotype limited view of people based on false ideas about them

sub-Saharan Africa part of Africa south of the Sahara Desert

tax money that the government collects from people and businesses in order to finance the running of the country

trade buy and sell goods

treason to take actions against, or be disloyal to, your own country

United Nations (UN) international organization made up of most countries. It promotes world peace and development.

urban relating to town or city life

Western ideas and ways of doing things that come from the United States and Europe

Find Out More

Books

Bowden, Rob. *Africa South of the Saraha.* Chicago, Ill.: Heinemann Library, 2008.

Domingo, Vernon. South Africa. Philadelphia, Pa.: Chelsea House, 2004.

Gritzner, Jeffrey A. *North Africa and the Middle East.* New York, N.Y.: Chelsea House, 2006.

Solway, Andrew. *Africa.* Chicago, Ill.: Heinemann Library, 2008.

Websites

Africa Aid
www.africaaid.org
This website explains about some of the current **aid** programs in Africa to support health, education, water, and the **economy**.

BBC World Service
www.bbc.co.uk/worldservice/africa/features/storyofafrica
This site explains the history of Africa and its people.

Office of the Special Advisor on Africa
www.un.org/africa/osaa/
This United Naions website tells about important initiatives in Africa, including links to the New Partnership for Africa's Development (NEPAD) and others.

PBS Africa for Kids
http://pbskids.org/africa/
Learn about kids in Africa from kids living there and learn some activities related to African culture.

Places to visit

Many museums have good collections of African art and culture. Here are some examples:

Museum for African Art
36-01 43rd Avenue at 36th Street
Long Island City, NY 11101
Tel: (718) 784-7700
www.africanart.org

National Museum of African Art
Smithsonian Institution
P.O. Box 37012 MRC 708
Washington, DC 20013-7012
Tel: (202) 633-4600
http://africa.si.edu

The Museum of African Culture
13 Brown Street
Portland, ME 04101
Tel: (207) 871-7188
www.africantribalartmuseum.org

Index